SARA BUTLER

Waiting For A Change

It's cold and miserly outside and the
light's already slacking off, but read-
ing Waiting For A Change feels like
sitting in a warm kitchen with a drink
in your hand and Sara Butler by your
side, and you're listening to Sara talk,
her voice is all her own, and you can
open your heart to it: the sudden sad-
ness, the smiling affirmations, the
movement from now to then and back
again.

Deborah Harvey

Contents

Foreword

It has been an enormous privilege to be entrusted with Sara Butler's poems. As editors we have been moved and amazed anew by Sara's deft turn of phrase, sharp wit and vivid observation. A life truly and fully lived and a warm and rich memoir it is a joy to share.

Editors: Morag Kiziewicz and Ama Bolton

Acknowledgement

Without the initiative and enthusiasm of friends and fellow writers Mo Kiziewicz and Ama Bolton this collection might have languished in dusty folders or been buried in the digital haystack forever. Profound thanks are due to them for their devotion to the project.

Other champions of Sara's poetry have been Colin Brown and Deborah Harvey of The Leaping Word, Bristol. Thanks also to Sue Boyle in Bath, Anna Garry at UEA and the Fountain Poets in Wells.

None of this would have been possible without the dedication, love and support for Sara from Bob Spode.

1

Childhood

Bishopston, Bristol

I was born there, spent my childhood there – in a big old Victorian house. It seemed to be full of rooms, freezing in the winter. My sister and I would get undressed for bed downstairs in front of the fire and then run like mad things clutching our hot water bottles up and up to the attic; then we'd jump into bed, pull the blankets over our heads until we could hardly breathe. But the consolation was that in the morning the window was magic – covered in exquisite patterns made by Jack Frost that stayed there most of the day if the temperature was really low. I could never work out how he did that.

Clevedon, Somerset

Our grandparents lived near the sea front and my sister and I would stay with them in the holidays. In the morning my Gran would just open the front door and we'd race over the Green to the shoreline and the heaving Bristol Channel with its misty outlines of Cardiff and Newport. When it was warm enough, we'd go swimming in the old pool, jump off the high board, nearly winding ourselves as we hit the water. We'd swim a few lengths, come out with mud slicks clinging to our chins, our baggy costumes.

Filton

Home of my other grandparents and the BAC and at the time I'm thinking of, my father working on Concorde, flitting between the UK and Toulouse – the prestige, the long hours, the pressure. There were always tales of the 2nd World War too when I was a child –although the air-raid shelter in the garden had long since become a potting shed.

May Day 1955

Five children squinting into the sun,
one wearing butterfly wings,
she's smiling at the camera
and her skirt has rucked up
so you can see her knickers.
It's her birthday and she's six.

There's a heatwave
and they're all starting to wilt,
the only boy is balancing
on his scooter, scowling.

On the grass in front of them
Cinders the black retriever
has keeled over onto her side
and Toby the tortoise is making
yet another break for freedom
that will end sadly.

In a minute Uncle Joe
will say, let's take a few more
for your granny while the sun's out.
The boy will throw down his scooter
and stomp off.

The girls will do as they're told.

Not Sleepy?

You want to stay awake
Right then
I'll make sure you do.
I wasn't but three or four,
every time my head nodded
he shook me.

I saw him years later in a dream,
sobered, alone
standing in a walled garden
white light
no shadows.

He looked up
caught my eye.

Wink

The house was Victorian
dark rooms big furniture
heavy curtains;
the sitting room silent.
A wedge of sunlight has got in
specks of dust float up and down.

My grandmother is asleep
she is having forty winks.
I am standing nearby
sucking my thumb
looking at her in great detail.
She has soft cheeks rosy
I can see the downy hairs
the mole above her lip
and best of all
there is a secret bobble
behind her ear just like a raisin.
Sometimes she lets me touch it.

I move closer and closer
lean over the arm of the chair
take my feet off the ground.

'Nana', she opens an eye.
'How many winks have you had?'
'Twenty'. The eye closes.

Percy

He'd run off when he was fifteen.
Left the farm, got a boat to Canada.
It was his aunt gave him the money.
They were filled with the same dreams.
He got a job as a stoker on the railways.
All those tales he'd tell of the Indians,
huge camps packed up, gone overnight.
No sign of their passing, just silence.
We'd sit in the front room having tea,
he always sat on his own, had a low
chair and a small table by the hearth.
If the weather was good he'd pick up
his binoculars, say who's coming to the
beach, see if we can spy a banana boat
chugging up the channel.

Football

All the way there he'd hold
my numb fingers tucked inside
his warm grip.
He'd walk I'd trot.
Saturday afternoon
up to the Downs
to watch the football.

November, grizzly,
mean-spirited,
the sort of miserly damp
that filters right into you,
no amount of stamping feet
could bring them back to life.

Best bit came
when someone got hurt
and the whole game
stopped and there was
a stretcher
and if I was lucky
an ambulance too and just
for a moment,
I'd think
we might
be going
home.

Speed

All of us kids squeezy
in the back seat screaming
faster faster,
the old black Citroen
streaming along
Jimmy Jones
pushing his foot right
down to the floor
the needle creeping up
us kids screaming,
nearly wetting
ourselves.

Someone told me later
he'd once killed a child,
an accident.

I imagined her running;
racing down a path
just for the hum of it
wind in her hair,
laughing and laughing,
a voice behind her calling
mind that road now
Jessie, will you
mind that road.

Assembly

We'd file into the silent hall all dressed the same – white ankle
socks, Clarks sandals, striped cotton skirts, white blouses.

She'd come in
walk to the front
her head held slightly
to one side as though
God was having
a quiet word in her ear.

We'd sing a hymn and then there'd be a murmuring that grew
louder and wider as we lowered ourselves wriggling into a space.
She'd wait for silence.

One time
as we all stood to file out,
a girl in front had been betrayed
by that scarlet stain;
how we all looked away
for the shame of it,
glad it wasn't us,
left her to Miss Grayling
who whisked her off
to First Aid.

Shadows

He was moving in
after all those years with her,
he was joining them
getting a bedroom
meals downstairs. The men
had hauled and heaved
cajoled and flattered
the elderly furniture
up the stairs and round
to the landing, then settled
it in a darkening room.
A girl stands outside the door
turns the handle.
In the cracked mirror
on the opposite wall
a shadow slowly moving,
the cool air sweetly scented
is sickly, familiar.

There isn't anything there
I've had a look. It'll be your
grandmother's perfume,
Dior, she loved it, chucked
it about all over the place,
it'll be in the wood.
Don't say anything
to your Grandad.

Archie

He was a young man then,
worked on the family farm
up before dawn each day
moving from one essential task
to the next, then on to the next
and full circle: a continuous rhythm
day in, day out, minor changes
in the harvest, minor changes
in the milk yield, minor changes.

Then 1914 and a rare opportunity.
He volunteers, joins the navy
ends up on a submarine -
hiding in those ice-cold depths
hunting down the enemy
always on edge for the same hit,
his own finale.

My mother remembered visiting
when she was young
and he, seemingly an old man already,
spent most of his days by the fire,
mainly silent, war wounds still
painful, still not healing.
He'd call in the old collie,
roll up his trouser leg.
That dog would lick and clean,
lick and clean,
do the healing for him.

Clevedon Pier

Racing, the two of us
flat out to the bit where the planks
had pulled apart leaving a gap,
bit of spit in the air
mucky old Bristol Channel
heaving below.

We'd lie face down
peering through
the chinks
scouting for wreckage,
once saw a shop dummy
a woman naked
rising and falling
in the swell
trapped against
the cast iron pillars
one arm raised
in greeting.
What could you do?
Felt like
we'd been there
for ever willing her
to freedom
till the outgoing tide
nudged her on her way,
still waving.

Nailed

I longed to be like Annette.
I can even remember her surname.
Her Mum let her wear
flock nylon party dresses
to school and her nails were long
like the ones you saw
in pictures of fashion models.

When my gran was cutting mine
I asked her if she'd make them look the same.
She said I'd have to put up with
the ones I'd been given.

Troubles

Arm in arm walking down
the road the two of us,
early summer, me and Jean
coming back from town
on our way home.

When we get there the door
flies open while she's still
rummaging about for the key
and then he's shouting 'where've
you bloody been?' shoves her
half way down the hallway
she falls into the radiator picks
herself up brushes something off her shoulder
like it's just a speck of dust
totters along to the kitchen
puts the kettle on, shuts the door.

'I didn't mean to do that,
you hear me?'

Metamorphosis

Saturday morning was swimming lessons down at the baths –
the stench of chlorine her old costume, baggy, misshapen, and
even though it was her brother who said 'who'd want
to look at you' it mattered. Mr Shawner towed her up and down
in a halter shouting
'nearly' 'almost there' 'that's it' but it never was.

This Saturday though as she gets out of the water
and goes to change
she sees a kingfisher blue costume
twinkling on the wet tiles
and slips it on
it's slinky, clings to the skin.

She makes her way to the diving platform
feels taller, older, undoes her ribbon
so that her hair tumbles loose,
up the steps she climbs
and the whole world beneath her
goes quiet.

She walks to the end of the high board
stands there her toes curling over the edge
sees all these upturned faces, their mouths wide open
and then she springs
dives
enters the water
like she was born to it.

2

Mother

Thread

The clacking of needles,
a dropped stitch hidden
within the warmth of wool.
I pick and turn things
cling to the thread
as it spins out
runs the length of an arm.

My mother would have
understood this a different way,
found her own world
buried deep inside,
one that I have only
seldom glimpsed.

This other kind of skype

How strange,
there we'd been saying goodbye,
you in New Zealand, me over here
slight distortion,
when just at that moment
somehow or other
we seemed to be sailing
across the kitchen floor again
leaving behind the snow bound garden,
the ancient pear tree groaning out its song,

our mother has upended
the old table onto the lino floor
its splintery legs facing due south
we are set fair for other worlds,
tea towels make up the sails
we have water
we have cake
we have a mast flying
an old silk scarf.
A breeze has got up
we're standing in the prow
hands to our foreheads,
shielding our eyes
from the glare, squinting
right into the horizon.

Did you see?

Photograph 1946

1950, a dank flat seething with trouble.
In the kitchen a wary child
kneeling on a chair
peers through the rungs, senses
her father's ill-temper
the sullen word,
the brittle snap
her mother's distance
as she turns from him
turns to the window
lost in dreams of
that one-time world.
Love carried in on the
back of wartime,
the seductive scent of survival.

Here they are in 1946,
a damp day in Dunster
leaning against a bridge,
the distance between them
already palpable,
a dry space held between
finger and thumb.

Percussion

He played Latin American music
with some of his mates.
There's a photograph of them
with Salvador Dali moustaches,
slicked back greased hair,
a bit of a swagger.

He'd spend hours beating
out the rhythms
on the kitchen table;
sometimes if he got fed up
he'd use the drumsticks on us,
you'd never quite know whether
it was a game or not. He did that,
changing something that was fun
into something that was not.

He didn't have a stop button; he'd make us
stamp up and down to the music he was playing
till the neighbours downstairs started banging
on the floor from below and he'd say *go on,*
jump, jump, stamp, stamp, let's really give them
something to bloody complain about.

But she came from another planet,
singing in *The Pirates of Penzance*
down at the local secondary school.
She'd practise while she was cooking
and we'd be the audience clapping.

The evening rehearsals got her
out of the flat. She'd run along
the pavements on the way home,
fast as she could
so she'd get back on time,
humming all the way.

Overheard

Don't touch her
like that again
no matter
the provocation –
that percussion
of slap on skin
the raised voices.

I lie here one wall apart
hands clenched
breathing too hard
all that misery
within spitting distance.

Next morning there's
you her and me
and silence sitting
cross-legged
between us.

Breakfast

two kids eating porridge
two eggs in a pan
a woman yawning flips them over
forgets the time forgets the toast

delivers the eggs on an icy plate
the eggs wait
shrink into themselves

the man yells
the plate hits the floor the kids cry
the woman sighs

I just wanted them sunny-side up

the woman wipes the table
kisses the kids
the man picks up the broken pieces
they sit together after the fallout

I'll make breakfast tomorrow

Hard Times

When things are on the cusp, when disorder shadows
the house, there is a dark struggling to get the words lined up
so they will not cause alarm, will not go out of orbit, she writes
a letter:

My Dear,
*   I have. been*
*   through thehouse*
their are things
from
43
diffrent countries
I have
catulogged
them
*   all.*
*   love Ella*

On the back of the envelope a postscript:
bananas from equador
*   thi s week.*

A friend drinking coffee at the kitchen table
asks if it's in code.

Grounded

You see, she's been brought up quite short
in the way that you can be,
left with the feeling of getting caught
in a world where she might seem
much the same but keeps going off
to this or that or the other extreme
in some ways it's hilarious
but today things got tough
and the results were so various
that even her sister said enough was enough
so today she's at home
cutting up rough
says she's always alone,
and there's no-one to phone.

Hearing Voices

They get a hold of you
voices
they can slow right down
enunciate
e a c h w o r d
or embark
on a crowded chatter that mimics
a murmur of starlings.

Sometimes the voices
came from Mars
and I would find her
by an open window
head held
to one side
like a small bird listening,
finger to her lips
shhh .....
message from
a spaceship,
it's coming this way.

Absence

He's been waiting
for weeks you see,
just wanting to know,
just that. Some days it's like
someone's got his heart
in a grip so tight
he can hardly breathe.

And then a letter comes, he reads it out –
it says she can come home for a few days,
see how it goes.
He reads it twice more, puts it in his pocket,
next thing
he's out in the garden
getting the lawn mower out;
he just flies up and down, faster and faster
his old jacket flapping
in the breeze
revving it round the corners, nearly airborne

you can hear him whistling,
same old tune;
he always gets that last bit wrong.

Visiting Hours

At night, she whispers,
they creep
down that corridor
and get into the cupboards
they are all lawyers,
about this she is quite clear
she has seen them.

Her fingers knead the sheet
the restless movements
on and on.

Is that my lovely?

It'll be dark

I'd get home, one time
all the doors
all the windows
wide open
my shirts, pyjamas
her undies, the sheets
all hanging there
catching that slow breeze;
like we were just having
an airing day,
like we lived in Spain,
and the furniture
all moved about
even the old dresser,
like she'd found a strength
worthy of Goliath,
this purge.
What's it all about, all this?
What were you thinking of?
There she'd be at the altar rail
half-undressed,
kneeling and keening
keening and kneeling
her arms held up for mercy.
Shall we get your clothes on?
Shall we be walking home?
You and me together;
it'll be dark.

Bad Traffic

These last days
a disconnection,
things go unrecognized.
You leave the house
walk down the path
move out into toytown,

a green bus
a yellow sun
a white sky.

Where the kerb edges the road
you take one slow-time
step into the mess of traffic,
then another one,
each one echoing more
than the one before.

The traffic heaves to,
winds down a window
sees you
your cotton skirt lifting
in the hot breeze,
lower yourself
softly onto
the whispering tarmac,
nestle between the wheels
of a car and a truck,
supine.

Edmund

I never knew this
until just before she died
or how long she'd kept
it to herself -
that there had been a lover
before the war
and despite those four years,
he had come home.

It was no good, she said,
too much damage.
Your grandfather now,
he was a kind enough man.

Searching for Someone

Dusk and the streets slip by.
Would you remember the way
to Horfield prison now, right next
to the school? – us kids would
chuck stones over the walls. We'd
go swimming down at the Baths
lunch-time, buy chips on the way back,
reeking of chlorine.

Those streets, Victorian houses
heavy, secret, so many bells to push

on the front doors now. It was number
55. A laburnum tree in the front
garden once came down in a storm
half burying poor old Caitlin
in its thick branches, its golden yellow flowers.

The street lights musty orange
in the evening mist, where are you?
I have knocked on so many doors
slid back so many bolts, peered inside.
Berkley Road, Shadwell Road, Egerton
Road. A number 45 bus goes by;
you are not on it.

I get to the Gorge late, go the way
we would have walked, come out on
the Downs near Ladies Mile and then over
the grass to the Suspension Bridge.
We'd hang over the side looking at the cars
moving along the Portway below,
just like dinky toys.

End of the day and I'm nearing Clevedon,
Lady Bay with its slipway, its pebbly beach
that salty tang. The pier reaches out
into the Bristol Channel, a misty shadow.

Old moon rising shivers on the incoming tide,
a figure by the shoreline disappearing.

You wouldn't wait, would you?

3

Relationships

Cuts

He says he can't eat it and why
does she cook this way when he can't?
He sits crumpled at the table
his old hands holding
a knife and fork,
despair rising.

She sits down hard as cheese rind
watching him chew
listening to his damp chewing
thinks she might erupt out of her seat
and disappear through the ceiling like
a fighter pilot pressing the ejector button.

They sit opposite each other

caught in the white glare of the strip
lighting above, her in a green jumper
with penguins lined up across the front
and him all camouflaged in grey,
the only sounds the scrape of cutlery
on plate and that wet chewing,
he's watching her too, sees the way she
runs her tongue across her front teeth
trying to free the bits of food
pulling her jaw about.

Funny that at this moment
him with a fork halfway to his mouth
and her with her face all distorted
that the power goes. There they are frozen
in darkness as if a black flash
photograph's been taken of the two of them.

For a moment no-one moves
then she's feeling her way towards a candle
and he's fishing in his pocket for his lighter,
they look at each other
marooned in candlelight
the room all disappeared in shadow,
she looks softer he thinks and smiles.

She leans across the table, brushes
his old face with her hand,
it's alright Jack –
you've got gravy on your chin.

Brief Encounter

Got to Plymouth
missed the connection
sat in a worn out waiting room
its automatic door behaving badly
every time anyone moved
it flung itself open in a tantrum
an icy wind forcing its way in.

Old man sitting opposite rocking
backwards and forwards chanting
I'm so cold
I'm so cold

He turns to the woman next to him
shouts:
what
are you
going to do
about it?

She gets up,
leans over him
I'm going to the Ladies
where you can't come.

I know where you're going

Go on, look back.
I'm on the opposite side of the road
got my hood up
go on, look behind you,
that's it,
did you see me?
did you?
You know who I am
don't you? Even though
you'd rather you didn't.

You're walking a bit faster,
mind you don't slip,
oh, those pavements are icy
and it's another fifteen
minutes or so, isn't it?
and it's getting darker.

I'm still here –
getting a bit worried, are we?
bit uncomfortable?

You'll take the next turning
left off Ringstrasse, I know you will.
When we get there,
you'll push open the door,
walk across the cobbles,
start to climb those dark
and winding stairs.

You'll get half-way up,
then you'll hear that heavy door
open and close again,
footsteps.
Will you think it's me
gliding up those stairs
behind you,
like an eel?
Will you?

I gave him a book

Christmas day
we stayed in the flat,
he'd got so drunk the night before

he was sick all morning.
We had to tell his mum and dad
he'd caught something
off someone else
and was a bit out of sorts

and could they postpone Christmas dinner
till the next day, we didn't want to miss it.

The book I'd given him
was a book about knots –
he spent all that Christmas
practising.

Bath Time

One evening both tired
they slip into the bath, steam
so thick
the walls are running
the mirror's in a fog.
She gets in
wriggles her way
between his legs
yawning and sleepy
leans back against him
skin all prickly in the heat
water lap lapping
lazy talking
lazy smiling,
think they could be anywhere,
a tropical orchid house
gasping for air.

Then she skews herself round
so as to see his face
and just for a moment
this icy chill
needles through the heat
intercepts, but she laughs
pushes it to somewhere else.
In all this warmth
things like that do not happen,
not here.

Tricky

I mean, I'll take him a cuppa
he'll say, what colour d'you call that?
I'm not drinking that gnat's piss
and you can feel the Arctic blast
from his armchair
right out in the kitchen.

When I was younger
he'd never have got away with it
I was wild then -
I'd go out with the bloke
two doors down to pay him back
get home real late
say I'd been round Sheila's
but I hadn't of course.

One time he knocked me
all down the hallway
to the back door. I fell against
the radiator, broke a tooth.

I don't know what it is about him,
he was always tricky
black hair blue eyes
leather jacket motorbikes
and there was the sex,
it'd never been like that before,
then curled up like two spoons
all night, my feet warm against his.

Kitchen Dancing

He sidles round the table,
so, he says, got another man,
have you?
Me, I'm as quick
as a mirror carp
vanishing in deep water –
I side-step to the right
he side-steps after me
he chassés to the left
I chassé to the right,
two steps this way
two steps that way
then he leans forward
face like a fuchsia
breath heaving out
like an old pair of bellows –
you're a very attractive
woman my dear.
I pirouette to the door
and I'm out before he knows it.

Not as light on his feet
as he thought.

Moon Walk

A bitter night
snow from the east
the house numb.
A woman checks how she looks
leaves by the side door.

A misty moon
full and tender
slips through cloud
lights the pollard oak
the fallen willow.

The woman treads softly
keeps in against shadow
skirts the barn
flits down the track
to a car
gently throbbing,
a door slinks open
and she slides in,
tyre tracks
left in the moonlight,
three dark drops
on the drifting snow.

Drift

Cattle pushing and shoving
trying to find a bit of shelter,
snow as thick as porridge
sticking to the old barn doors.
Flakes blowing stronger,
getting more powerful start whirling
and spinning out of a pewter sky.

She's come up to feed the cattle,
trudged half a mile in the heavy snow
eyes burning in the northerly gale;
it's all she can do to stand
upright. She lifts armfuls of hay
into the racks, the cattle shifting
from one hoof to the other, pushing
her about as though they're trying
to get a bargain in the autumn sales.

Then she looks up, peers into
the jagged eye of the storm
sees this distant figure bent double
hardly visible, old coat flapping
so hard like he's about to take off.
She can hear him calling,
"Are you alright, Henny?
I've been looking for you all over."

When he gets there he puts an arm
round her shoulder tells her she looks
like an angel even in this weather.
He'd come to help but she shrugs
him off like he's the last person
in the world she'd need help from.

Me and Lil

We were talking about men,
not those tidied-up ones
with their corners
all folded in neat
but men we'd loved;
bad men in their
old leather jackets
with the collar turned up
a fag on the go
a sniff of danger.

Lil was just getting
to the bit about Arnie –
do you know she says,
when he takes
his clothes off at night
sparks fly out.

Picnic

Now that we've said
too much,
let's take the picnic
down to the river anyway,
we could walk downstream
to where the water shallows
see if the dipper's still there.

Here, he says,
a cheese sandwich for you
and one for me,
a boiled egg,
two rosy pears
and a glass of wine.

A passing mallard drifts across
looking for crumbs.

I didn't mean it you know.

Becalmed

white sky
pale sun
pine trees
the way they settle,
their roots flexing in the dunes,
small lake rounded
little grebe diving
small boat
two people reclining
the woman leaning
back into the man
water shadowing
small shiver
passing through

Small Talk

She's such fun,
seems like she's on her own kids to bring up
partner disappeared.

I watch you getting ready
checking the way you look, in the mirror
you won't catch my eye look away.

A dinner party
small intimate
pats of butter
on coloured tiles
a bowl of nasturtiums
crystal wine glasses thin stems
the room already too hot,
small talk
a joint of pork skewered.

She comes in late
blonde petite laughter
slides into the chair next to you
hand on your sleeve asks for water,
absorbs you.

Sunday Breakfast

Two nice eggs
brought in from the cold
one as pale as marble
the other walnut brown

crack them
on the pan's edge
fry them
till they're done
eat them with
some toast and butter
eat them till they're gone

we're alright then,
aren't we?

4

Creatures

Pembrokeshire

Along the track I dip down into
bramble
sloe
hawthorn,
sun up high on the ivy
red admirals
feeding in the last
of the summer's warmth
their wings flattened
as they bask.

I'm so close

I could stroke them.

Birder

Once met this man
stringing a net
across the river Yare
late spring,
he was ringing swifts.

Standing thigh deep
he shows me one up close.
See this, he says, and parts
the feathers,
flat flies
as big as your thumbnail.

All night I could feel them
scuttling, sucking blood.

Hare

A gentle lane
edges out
slips along contours,
rolls down between
deep hedges
reaches the cross-roads,
melts in.

An SUV with gaping grill purrs out its rhythm
and as the gates hum open spits the gravel and is gone,
a metal cocoon surfing the tarmac.

But what of the hare
the fractured hare
elbowing her broken way
towards the verge
and the wide wide field
where her leverets crouch
in their shallow forms?

Their tension
grips bone and muscle
tight and tighter.
They wait
and wait
and wait.

Heron

See how he parachutes in
between the dripping alders
the bank of willow,
comes down vertically
feet first braking all the way
then turns to stone
pretending he's not there
that he's not after the loved-up frogs
those purring males
out cruising for the ladies,
last thing they're thinking about
is a grey assassin.

Kittiwakes

Gingerly progressing
along the cliff edge,
north-west coast of Sutherland,
slippery-stoned, little grip;
you out bird-ringing,
maybe not so gingerly.
Watched you one time
ringing swifts that flew
astonished into a net strung across the river Yare.
Either way, this time
your grip was lost and you fell –
man flying
man falling
from those dark cliffs.

August

Sometimes on an
ordinary afternoon
day-dreaming in the heat
your china teacup
filled with ambrosia
that sense of luck
that all is well;
and then a sliver of memory
tacks its way in
from nowhere in particular
interrupts
and there you are
in a long-lost garden
August, bleached
watching
a stoat
shadow a rabbit
eating it slowly
from the back
of the neck.

Making a living

You'd maybe have to wait a while
before you saw them,
dusk, a cool mist rising
hunkered down in the long grass,
river Yare slipping by.

They'd edge out of their burrows
whizz down the mud slides
into the water, dive, disappear.
Coypu, you might see the odd ripple,
see them surface, checking you out.

Non-native, they were caught in cage-
traps and shot, then just when
it looked like they'd all gone
those wily old trappers would open
the cages instead and let them go.

Kept themselves in work for years.

One for sorrow

Two magpies in a trap
hidden in a darkening copse
one the lure, the other lured.

Silent, wary,
they tap at wire
find the boundaries of their cage
and isolated, withdraw
into imprisonment.

Comes a man
through birch and cherry
gentle green,
moves in shadow through the thicket
past tangled briar and muddied rut,
lifts out the lure
eyes that deep and knowing eye,
the black silk shot through with blue
and beats it hard
against a sycamore trunk,
then tosses it away.

With bloodied hand
he turns to the trap
and gently feeds the lured.

pica pica

Pond

What do you see
when you peer down there
part the bulrush
glide through pondweed
digits webbed
limbs trailing,
watch out for the nymphs
carnage and mayhem
deceptive nymphs
with their hooked lips
impaling
nymph the impaler
tadpole impaled
years of hunting
down in the depths
mud dark and slimy
detritus deep
nowhere to hide
from this hawker

mirror carp
slides by
barely a ripple

Raven

A raven squats
at the top of the cypress.
Heavy old head
sooty old beard
hunkered right down
fixes his deep eye
on the horizon
cranks open that boot black beak
sucks in a cool south-westerly
an ash tree
two barns and the Robertsons
draws it all down
into his dark interior
then chokes out
this bellowing call
that lifts and carries
as far as the Blackdown Hills:

A l l t h i s i s m i n e.

Rescue

A herring gull on the roadside
beak all caught up in plastic
a Tesco label hanging on.
Got the plastic off with wire cutters
took him home in the van.

Two days he spent there,
luxury accommodation
clean water, egg and milk
shit everywhere.
Second night he was perching
on one leg, head tucked
under a wing.

Let him fly the next day
thought he'd be gone so fast
but he spent thirty minutes
preening every feather,
meticulous,
flew when he was good and ready.

Sexton Beetle

You may think
you perform feats
of great courage
when overwhelmed
by a trolley
in Tesco's,
but spare a thought
for the sexton beetle
the size of a thumb nail,
shoulder to the wheel
heave-ho-ing
a fresh carcass,
a bank vole,
to the safety
of its subterranean lair.

The laying of eggs
that follows,
the fending off of foes,
the shoring
up for winter,
the long
long
wait for spring.

Chicken

This is the kindest
way to do it –
a sharp twist.
But my grandmother
wasn't always right
and Joey the cockerel
ran around
for five minutes
his head abandoned
in the dirt
his white feathers
weeping blood.

Now we pluck him,
not like that,
hold Joey
this way round
give the feathers
a firm pull
away from you,
that's it,
pinch up the flesh
a quick snip,
now slide your hand
in all the way

grasp those
slippery innards,
and ease them out –
a glistening treasure trove,
sunshine yellow
purple, brown
streaks of scarlet
tumbles out.

Aged six, I had no idea
Joey had it in him.

Scrumping

Blackbirds on wet grass
foraging for fallen apples
hold their heads to one side
looking, listening.
Swift lunge
into the rotting heart.

Seal pup

If you stand here
on this crumbling edge
peer down
into the rough gash
to the thin bay
where blackened boulders
are tumbled and heaped
against the cliff,
you'll see the pup
all creamy fur
wedged in against wet rock
lying on its back.
Its mother close in
treads water in the heavy swell
eyes us on the path above.
The pup raises a flipper
we wave back.

5

Sea

Drogheda

I know this place,
this passage tomb
these silent stones
this corbelled roof
and the sun
that finds its way

to the heart of things.

Hartland

You know that feeling
when you're by the sea
the world gone home
a lonesome beach.
Maybe it's September
the light starting to soften
seaweed gently rocking
in the pools
the mudstone slabs
stacked one to another
catnapping on the sand,
a silky sunset –
and then the first trickle
of a turning tide
fingers its way in, unhurried
insidious.

There's a cairn
rock and pebble
chest high
built on the shoreline.
Six of us then.

Two nights it lives through
swollen breakers,
the cut and tear of shingle
sucked back,
on the third night
something barely seen,

swift deadly
slips across the bay,
a riptide
hits it sideways on
lays waste.

Hinkley point

Power station up and running
grey sea grey noise

spotlight sweeping to and fro
sears the mist breaks the dark

jet plane loaded passing through
dips its wings disappears

two kids on the seas edge
fold their chairs paddle in

how long before a fault kicks in
how come we never see it coming

Tipping point

A man walks the line,
keeps to the track
whose blistering heart
ticks and heaves
beneath
his feet.

He carries a pack,
a stick,
traverses the westerly
spine of fjord
and mountain,
holds true to that line
through thickening cloud
and darkling sky
as it noses
and nudges
far beneath the crust,
fidgets against
a spur
feeling its way
toward the east.

Each day
he covers fifteen miles.
He leaves temperate forest
with its gentle lichens
that hold no print

of heavy boot,
no sign of passing.

On the fifth day
he sits high above
a crackling crevice
and as he reaches
for his pack,
dislodges a small white
stone
that starts a fall,
a clattering, an echoing
within the scarred walls,
gathering speed
gathering strength –
then a barely
perceptible
pulse
pulse
pulse

Outing

All the way there
she's between my feet
in a brown plastic
container that looks like
something you might
keep pickled onions in.
When my sister has
to brake hard it falls over
and I say 'sorry Mum'
without thinking.

We're looking for
a place where she might sense
the tide coming and going,
keep an eye on the clouds,
somewhere you could still see
Flat Holm and Steep Holm.

When we get there
it's chosen itself,
a stretch of grassy cliff
stitchwort, campion
a tumble of black rock below.
We take handfuls of ash
some of it fine like dust
some of it pieces
heavier, darker, edged.

Let it all fly.

Polperro

There are eight of them, coastguards' cottages
all lined up along the top
of the hill. You can still walk
into the lookout in one of them
just by lifting a latch.

Imagine a time when everything
depended on them,
how they might have sat there
on and off for most of a lifetime
searching for signs of smugglers,
for ships caught out in wild storms,
familiar with almost every part
of the ocean's wayward temper –

the way a sea fret
can move inland
just like that,
hide the world;

no warning.

North Norfolk 2014

You skirt the Corsican pines
and then you're out
the beach wide open
the shore a distant shiver
sand whipping
your ankles
you can see
where February's storms
poured into the dunes,
along to the west
dark footprints uncovered
by violent seas
800,000 years old,
a group of five hominids
moving north
to south
appear
disappear.

Crawl

You followed him down
to the shoreline
remember?
The tide coming in fast
raw undisciplined,
your skirt blown
wet between your legs
eyes straining
in the white light
searching.

He'd swum out
through the heavy surf
dividing the breakers
like Moses.

You see him
in and out
of the oily swell,
he turns his head
to breathe
one arm over
then the other
turns to driftwood
turns
breathes.

6

Norfolk

Southburgh, Norfolk

Heavy snow in January blowing in on a sharp north-east wind. Me, out in my wellies and your old overcoat carrying hay into the barn to feed the cattle, filling up the racks. Their warmth gentle round me, their breath rhythmic, their cudding. I'm out there breaking the ice on the water trough when I hear a voice calling my name. I peer down the track in the thick snow and then I'm smiling and laughing as the vicar trudges into view – the only visitor I'd had for days and he'd battled his way through all the drifts just to see if I was ok.

Runhall, Norfolk

A red brick cottage, everything symmetrical rather like a picture in a child's book. It was meant to be happy; a place to live well in. It was neither of those things. It was breakdown and break up and sour days and nights with all the fizz lost and gone and that exhilaration for change tempered with a slice of grief. In the end you loaded up your old van and shot down the lane like a bullet. Phew!

Keswick, Norfolk

One time we lived in a flat in the Mill House – a big old place riddled with damp and peeling plaster. It was right next to the water mill and the river Yare that flowed almost past our door. The miller had been born there and had worked there all his life. One winter when the temperature fell well below freezing, he opened the sluice gates to flood the grazing meadows so that they'd freeze. We skated over grass, people came from nowhere with their old skates and we were out there all day making out we came from another time.

Southburgh

a small church, squared flint work
the spire heading heavenwards
mid Norfolk, wide horizons
autumn oaks, an easterly wind.
Come through the door with me,
It's bare, silent, a damp chill
nuzzles your skin

Keswick, Norfolk

We'd moved there early one summer,
a tiny hamlet at the end of a rough lane –
old clapperboard mill straddling the river,
a loose board hanging on high up
banging and banging in the breeze.

We had a flat there, the walls grew mould
the wallpaper peeled away, it was that damp.
House martins collected mud in the spring,
built their nests under the eaves.

In an ancient sheep hut hornets nested,
every summer they'd set out on a steady course
that never wavered, just like old aeroplanes.
You just needed to duck.

When the grazing marshes flooded, I'd wade
to work, the water sometimes up to my thighs
the odd rat swimming along, a bit of company.

In the end, we had to move, drove away in
a hired van, didn't dare look back. Dogs on
the back seat, ferrets in a wooden box.
Went to a square red brick house on a prairie
that looked like a child's drawing,
everything slightly out of kilter.

Water mill

Coming off the A11 I'm thinking how it might be now, narrowing
it all down,

wonder if you can still wade out mid-stream watch the water
pounding through the millrace,
d'you remember when the temperature went down to minus 15,
they opened the sluice gates
to flood the grazing marshes so they'd freeze,
we skated over grass, people came from nowhere.

When I get there it's a bit like I've not been away,
that's where I watched the kingfishers diving
and further along's where the cattle would wade in
on hot summer days when the flies were bad.

But the mill's all done up to the nines, two black Audis parked
outside and a sign –
No Waiting.

Lost

'Half-way down the thin lane,
turn down a track on your left,
you can't miss it', that's what he'd said.
Imagine it though in winter
the lane slicked with mud, running water,
that time of day when the light sneaks off early,
mist creeping in blurring the familiar.

Everything you drive by looms unknown
so you abandon the car, trudge along
till the track nudges your elbow
and something seems to say
'down here, down here'.

You stumble along the overgrown track
your leather boots slipping,
your tights snagging,
thinking what are you doing?
go back, go back...

But then a light jigs about
in the blackness
and a voice is near saying,
'what took you so long?'
and an arm round your shoulders
taking you in.

Road kill

It took both of us
to carry the carcass
from the car boot
to the kitchen table.
Rigor mortis had not yet
set in and the badger
was floppy
inclined to slide
onto a chair.
I remember
that when we investigated
the stomach contents
it was full of earthworms
still wriggling.

Some friends were coming
to dinner next evening
and we served badger steaks
cooked in burgundy
with thyme and marjoram.

They said it was
the best beef
they'd ever tasted.

Asylum seeking

Me and Lenny
standing together
passing the time of day.
It's late July
the wheat ripening,
a bit of reverence
the way we regard
this painted lady
soft landed
on sweet rocket –
all the way from Africa
flying low
her young won't last
the winter
and neither will she.

Lenny says
what does she
want to do that for?

It's a mystery

Harvest

Top meadow
cut and baled
mid June
the heat
throbbing,
the old barn
stuffed to the rafters
with sweet grass.

Two days and it's
hotting up,
night time all I'm
dreaming of is smoke
easing through,
flames devouring
dry timber,
spontaneous
combustion.

Early morning
George turns up –
you keep those old
barn doors shut,
that'll make good hay.

Early autumn, hedging ...

It's the bramble
that riots across
the narrow lanes
barring the way
with its dark green feelers,
its tearing thorns,
last of the blackberries
clinging on,
finding an intimacy
in which to hook and weave
the warp and weft.

Not long before
the way is barred,
the breaking tarmac
indistinguishable
from the rest.

Raising Beef

In a darkening field a bull calf slides
out of his mother into the long grass;
wet, membrane-clad exhausted.

He was black, rough-coated
he grew fast, he grew difficult
he grew into who he was,
you had to watch him
all the time
never turn your back.
Yet when he was ready
and I took him to the abattoir
he moved like a dream,
like he'd been there before,
down the ramp he sauntered
into the slaughterman's arms.

And me,
I betrayed him
for he trusted me
and I was not to be trusted.

Rhythm

First time I see Jimmy
I think he's an angel
up on the back of a trailer,
hair like barley straw
evening sun coming low
through the trees
giving him a halo.

I squint up at him
from the barn floor
and him, he's like a
pendulum
swinging his body from
side to side
lifting the bales
one by one
one by one
pitching them down
to the men below.

This rhythm
he says,
it gets a hold of you
and it stays.

Me, I think
I'd like a bit of that
rhythm too.

Scent

A billy goat senses a nanny goat
in season when she's just left home
in a secure car with the windows sealed.
She sends out messages
unconfined delicious overpowering.
When she arrives at the smallholding
he's all packed in behind high metal
gates and a wall waiting,
his upper lip pulled up to meet his nose
with the exquisite appearance of a sea anemone.
He flexes his shoulders, his flanks shiver
barges the gate and trots out,
master of secretions.

I know the flighty reek of a blackbird just before dawn
that makes an eyelid twitch, and long before
this year's swallows whooped across the dewpond
I knew they were coming, a sense of must in the air
made me stop, pinpoint direction,
miles away.

These days I seldom walk the Hangings,
a slope of pasture wet with the flow
of underground springs, it's the closet sweetness
of old bones that stops me, too close for comfort.

Fire

First the glow
then the outbreath,
flames seething
through the roof space
into the thatch above
where the draught fans up
a roaring
a thunder,
heat heat.
A snack becomes
a banquet.

The morning after
can you see the broken
chimney stack
halved and naked,
a torn curtain
caught against the brick
winding and unwinding
in an early breeze?
The old beams ashen scorched
send out smoke signals.
In a forgotten window
red geraniums
still dancing.

Singed

When the house burnt down
everything went –
clothes I'd lived in like a second skin
my old boots that could find my feet
in the dark.
It was like being naked.

Standing in Debenhams
looking at acres of clothes
I realized there was nothing
left to go with anything.

I bought a tight leather skirt
that came half-way up my thighs
some long scarlet boots
and a black velvet top that hugged
me half to death.

Naked

She'd been asking where
she could go for a pee,
it was midnight you see
and what with all the people
the house on fire
the other firemen all over,
the fields too dark
and the edges of the house
holding on to such shadow,
well, I said she'd be alright
in one-acre, no-one'd be going
in there, why would they want to
the cattle would be down
by the orchard. So she's just in there
pulling down her knickers when
someone turns the floodlights on.

I thought afterwards
that it can't have been
a mistake. The only woman
among all those men
in all that heat and destruction;

they were having a laugh.

Home

It's the way he comes
in from the cold
that does it,
that way he has
of coming home –
the boots left muddy
on the step
his old jacket
hung up on the door,
leaning back against the sink
the light catching,
telling me if the calf's
born yet.

What if?

This is
Where we were
One day
Travelling through France
Where blue-veined Roquefort cheeses
Squat on wooden racks
In the cool, dry caves.
This is where we were,
Wandering along, a hand's
Touch apart.

(Ah, what if we had known then?)

That explosion out of the
Darkness back into the sunlight.
Driving along through the sweet chestnuts
Sun-roof open to the skies.
All that smiling
All that loving
What if we had known?

The Sculptor's Stone

I watch him
as he does this –
pulls off his
goggles
and the mask,
puts down the
sander.
wipes his mouth
with the back of his hand,
shakes off the dust,
stands
back a little –
watches me.

I am pale as an early moon,
cold and smooth and
gently freckled,
I hold shadow,
I hold light,
I hold heat after dusk,
I fall silent in the cool,
night air.

He runs his hand
the full length of me,
his fingers
lingering over me,
rests his forehead
on mine.

Then
stands back a little,
smiles,
leaves me.

Footsteps

Nobody'd believe her of course
but one morning early
she thought he'd come back,
how else would you explain
the footsteps she'd heard
soft on the stone path that night
as she moved in and out of sleep,
or his old jacket that she'd cleaned
and put away, hung up
in the lean-to again,
damp from early morning rain.

Changes

He came round
asking if I'd sell
the field
almost as soon
as you were gone,
brought me a cheap
old bottle of red wine,
maybe he thought
that'd do the trick
that there'd be almost
anything I'd say yes to.

But that field
with its two
elderly walnut trees
holding each other up
limbs cracking
grey bark shedding
roots loosening grip,
it bordered a pond
kingfishers shot across
straight as a die
with their high-pitched
whistling -
it belonged.

Velvet

When I brush up against it
on the back of the door,
wear it again maybe months later,
I feel as though I'm home,
in the right skin,
the black velvet
fading like an old labrador
to a gingery brown
the pockets still hiding
those few flat pebbles,
skimmers
waiting for a calm sea.

Perspective

I shrink it all down
to a child's size:
a toy farm.

There's a house,
a barn.
a pond.

We'll have two ducks
on the pond
and two cows in the yard,
one is black
the other brown.
We'll have three chickens
hitching up their skirts
and running.

Over here
near the house,
we'll have a woman
with a trowel in one hand
and some sweet williams in the other;
two dogs lying on the grass
catching scents of fox,
rabbit, thyme
as they drift by.

We'll have a sun in the sky,
three clouds like ice-cream cones

and an old tractor
coming up the drive
pulling a trailer
stacked high with straw.
The man's wearing
a hat.

Just here
in a field
we'll have two old walnut trees;
a jackdaw nesting in this one,
a kestrel in the other;
and a kingfisher
diving for small fry
down at the far end
of the pond.

Now stand back
let go of it.

7

Somerset

Landscape – Chesterblade

Early February,
a winter sun edging
towards Maesdown.
Jackdaws wing their way
to the stand of beeches,
the hills tuck and pin
float away in the evening mist,
distant trees break up
smudging into the hedge line.
I am an apprentice Gulliver:
huge, benign. As tall as the
monterey cypress that
dwarfs the church.

Five paces to Dorset
before the dark seeps in.

Walking

Sunday and the first time for months you can walk up a hill
on dry roads. It's late February, the kids racing ahead through
the dark tunnel of steep wooded banks, the dog following, nose
down, caught up in a heady scent of badger, hare and fox. As we
reach the top of Smalldown, the land breaks wide open and we
come out into a late sun, the Iron Age Fort still perching there
with its steep ramparts its clear views of Somerset. On a good
day you can see Glastonbury Tor and you may get a glimpse of
Hinkley Point, misty in the distance - nearer than you thought,
not about to go anywhere else anytime.

Farming

The farm's changed and the village with it but
I can't complain. I'm an outsider who came
15 years or so ago, entranced by the Mendip hills
the views that catch you off guard, the way almost
no-one knows where it is. There was a dairy herd
then and all the routine that went with it; you could
set your watch by it. Now it's beef – young animals
bought in, reared in the sheds, put out to grass in the
summer, inside in the winter, waiting for the cattle
transporter to turn up; but there's something about
those vehicles that chills – maybe it's their size
or the way the cattle frightened at first, clatter up
the ramp in the end; a bit of poking and prodding,
shouting and yelling to get them gone, last time.

Summer 2012

The lane spawns a river
caramel, swollen,
pumping iron –

rain horizontal
rain torrential
daily rain
for the rain that
we are about to receive, may our water butts
be truly thankful.
Old rain bored
with this Atlantic darkness
squatting over the west,
lifts the drain covers,
drills its fingers
against the pane
with an orchestra
and a wind section
blowing through the gaps ...
Let me in.
The dogs, depressed
slink closer to the sodden earth.
They need a therapist
and so do I.
Oh for the dry and droughty
flat lands of the east.

Chesterblade

Late August
the purple lobelias
are out
tall straight-stemmed;
bumblebees
weigh down the lip
crawl right in.

September ...

Early morning and I come out sleepy,
not quite all there, hands round a mug of tea
to keep them warm; then see on the grass
a few shreds of wet leather that become quite
soon a small dark being that becomes
a serotine bat, grounded. I offer it water
it drinks, opens its eyes; they are tiny pinheads,
bright blue. I pick it up, place it in the palm
of my hand, carry it, so very gently to the
churchyard and the ancient yew trees;
hold it up face forward to the covering of ivy
clinging on to the trunk, watch as it attaches
itself and then leave it there hanging.
One hour later and it's flown ... magic...

November

November is a mournful month
neither gentle October
nor much blessed
with a hard frost
that can magic
a decaying garden into mystery.

Evenings grow short;
time
wriggles

downhill

into

darkness.

Seven Sonnets

I

He's out on the lane like last time hanging
about. *If I see that dog off the lead*
it'll get shot – I'm on a public road and
my dog's on a lead, mean old bugger.
It's autumn, hundreds of young partridge
arrive in crates, never seen a field, an oak tree,
a beater or a gun. They swarm reluctant to fly
hug the tarmac. I want to tell them there
isn't much time, fly, fly hard from this soured
land before the guns get here in
their 4x4s. Alfred's tower a closed
fist on the horizon, holds up an index
finger pointing to the heavens.
I'd like to know what he'd have thought .

II

What would he have thought -
a woman, thin skirt, bare legs, alone,
walking to the dew pond where
swallows flicker across the water,
a late September heatwave the sun
pinning her down where the lane narrows,
two badgers up against the bank
one dried out its coat sticking to the tarmac
like old brillo pads, the other bloated
heaving from within – maggots , tidying up.
Tidying up's what's always going on –
the nettles outside the churchyard sprayed,
the verges shaved, the fields rounded up
as soon as the cattle are moved on.

III

There's something about cattle
being moved on –
out in the fields I watch them early evening
a white sun settling behind Maesdown,
shifting their weight, cudding,
but you try sneaking past, a dog in tow,
and they're after you – no way you'd run as fast.
The livestock transporter squeezes
down the narrow lanes, eases into the yard
where they're waiting, the farmer is
like a conductor with an orchestra –
a few waves of the baton and they're up the ramp
the doors bolted. They're on the farm for
eighteen months or so, then they go to their deaths.

IV

These men went to their deaths too
but there's an unease here –
a small church, squared flint work
the spire heading skywards,
mid Norfolk, wide horizons, autumn oaks,
an easterly wind. Come through the door
with me. It's bare, silent, a damp chill
nuzzles your skin, you couldn't wear a coat
that would keep it out. In front of the altar
two tombstones early 19th century, two men
grieved to death by the same man –
the father of one, the grandfather of the other.
Outside, a muddled graveyard much of it tangled
in bramble and goosegrass, words fading.

V

It's grey November and the light's fading early
but you can still see the dark shadows
of the duck sheds squatting on the edge
of the village; as you get closer a rising babble
that never seems to quite reach its crescendo.
According to the website, they are free to roam
in light airy barns and have access to water
for bathing. This all seems most jolly – a little like
Jemima Puddleduck with her bonnet and basket
treading water with her mates in a large pond.
My mate Lenny does it. It's a way to make a living
but when I'm standing at the shed door
passing the time of day I just see denial
and there aren't any ducks bathing.

VI

This isn't a time for ducks bathing – a harsh cold spell
unkind to small creatures has moved in
and seems inclined to stay – everything freezes,
the central heating packs up the sheets feel like
they've come from a morgue. There's that leaden sort
of sky that seems to compress it all, makes it hard to
get moving and a blackbird dead by the backdoor.
Then there's a blue sky and a low sun comes out
and we're off to the frozen Broads and I have skates
on and I'm out there on Ranworth Broad like I do
this every day and I'm Hans Brinker and the silver
skates or in a novel by Tolstoy or competing in the winter
Olympics, until someone reminds me that Ranworth is tidal
and beneath the ice I hear the water sighing.

VII

No thick ice on the Levels but the water's high
and the ground waterlogged. Ham Wall almost dusk -
it's the starlings coming in to roost
we're here for and we're not the only ones.
Sometimes you get lucky – a flock coming down
among cattle, the grass black with them
becomes a Catherine wheel, peeling away
from the ground turning and turning.
The real birders stick together and they have inside
knowledge. The rest of us jiggle about wondering
where to look next. Tonight though a huge
murmuration makes for the reed-beds behind us,
a lone peregrine shadowing them out on the edge
like last time, hanging about for stragglers.

waiting for a change

Say it's late February
and we're outside on the bench
all pulled in
against the Atlantic heave,
the meanness of an ice-pick wind,
looking down the stretch of mist
the smudge of hill
and valley,
looking to where
land stirs against the sea.

What we're waiting for
is a chink,
the wink of a watery sun,
dance flies
starting a spring-time set,
the risky plunge
of a serotine bat
into the dark chill,
first stirrings
of a queen wasp.

About the Author

Sara Butler was born and raised in Bristol, enjoyed Bishop Road Primary and endured Colston Girls School before heading to Norwich to read European Studies, including a year in Vienna.

Following teacher training she worked in a language school and lived in rural Norfolk. Teaching was always part time so enough of the day could be devoted to her goats, dogs, ferrets and cows. In 2002 she moved back to the Westcountry and lives in a small village in Somerset.

Cover photo of Sara Butler by Bob Spode.

Waiting For A Change by Sara Butler

It's cold and miserly outside and the light's already slacking off, but reading *Waiting For A Change* feels like sitting in a warm kitchen with a drink in your hand and Sara Butler by your side, and you're listening to Sara talk, her voice is all her own, and you can open your heart to it: the sudden sadness, the smiling affirmations, the movement from now to then and back again.

A love for nature infuses these poems, though it's never romanticised, Sara having both an eye and an ear for the dark and the all too human. And there's always the laughing 'yes', and sexiness, and a desire for something better, which is found and made real in these poems.

Deborah Harvey

Milton Keynes UK
Ingram Content Group UK Ltd.
UKHW031834070824
446675UK00004B/53